Original title:
Tying Hearts Together

Copyright © 2025 Creative Arts Management OÜ
All rights reserved.

Author: Natalia Harrington
ISBN HARDBACK: 978-1-80586-032-7
ISBN PAPERBACK: 978-1-80586-504-9

Tethered Journeys

Two squirrels with acorns in tow,
Running in circles, oh what a show!
They tripped on a branch and fell in a heap,
Giggling together, not making a peep.

A dog and a cat in a tug-of-war,
Chasing their tails, who knew there was more?
With a leap and a bound, they both took a spin,
And ended up tangled, but wearing a grin.

Two friends with a bike, one pedaling fast,
While the other hangs on, hoping it'll last.
They nearly went flying, oh what a delight,
Yelling with laughter, they soared through the night.

A pair of red balloons on a windy spree,
Dancing together, floating carefree.
But one took a dip in a gooey surprise,
And burst on the pavement—what a silly demise!

Through all the chaos, it's clear to see,
Life's tangled moments bring joy and glee.
So here's to the ties that make each day bright,
Laughter and love in the wild, what a sight!

Knots of Connection

We're two loose ends, flailing wide,
With a twist or two, we'll collide.
Like shoelaces in a tangled race,
Let's laugh it off, we've found our place.

A picnic spread, crumbs in your hair,
You trip on a joke, I pretend not to care.
But secretly plotting, I'll weave and I'll spin,
Our knots of laughter, where love can begin.

Threads of Love Interwoven

Your socks in the dryer, my shirt on the floor,
Our habits a patchwork, like quilts we adore.
With each silly thread, let's craft a new tale,
Stitching together, we'll never derail.

We bicker like siblings, we tease and we jest,
But when you slip up, I love you the best.
These threads that we tangle make patterns so bright,
In this circus of chaos, you're my favorite light.

Embrace of Entwined Souls

You pull at my hair while we dance in the rain,
Like tangled-up vines with a touch of disdain.
But your laughter's a hug, wrapping tight around me,
In this ruckus of love, I feel so carefree.

With pizza and movies, our plans might unroll,
Yet somehow we fumble, that's just our goal.
So let's embrace this beautifully weird,
With each twist and turn, our path becomes cleared.

The Fabric of Us

In patterns of chaos, we play and we scheme,
A tapestry woven from each silly dream.
With pockets of laughter and sleeves full of cheer,
We stitch up our fun while the world disappears.

If life throws us threads, that's not such a fright,
We'll quilt our own comfort, soft and just right.
So here's to the stitches, the rips, and the frays,
Together we'll craft our fantastical days.

The Cloak of Affection

In a cloak made of laughter, we wear,
Wrapped in giggles, not a single care.
With pockets of joy, we gather delight,
Sharing secrets beneath the moonlight.

With socks mismatched, our style is bizarre,
Yet in our odd ways, we shine like a star.
Two peas in a pod, but which one is which?
Together we dance, and life feels like a pitch.

Interlace of Lives

We spin in circles, a whirlwind of glee,
Bumping our noses like it's meant to be.
Life's a game of Twister, we stretch and we bend,
My weird little partner, my quirky best friend.

In jigsaw puzzles, we fit with a laugh,
Missing pieces found in our silly giraffe.
With a wink and a grin, we glue it all tight,
Interlaced in chaos, we take flight at night.

The Heart's Embrace

With arms wide open, we catch falling stars,
On a trampoline of love, we bounce into cars.
Our ticklish ribcages hold giggles galore,
In this comedy sketch, we always want more.

Chocolate and rainbows, our favorite treat,
Dancing through puddles with silly wet feet.
We share an umbrella, a colorful sight,
In laughter's embrace, everything feels right.

Together in Each Step

Step by step, in mismatched shoes,
Tripping on jokes and silly good news.
In synchronized flails, we stride with a cheer,
With each goofy stumble, our bond grows clear.

Side by side in this wacky parade,
Dancing to rhythms that never will fade.
With laughter as glue, we stick like a stamp,
Together we frolic, forever our camp.

Eternal Knots

Two shoelaces crossed in a chat,
They laughed at their fate, just like that.
A squirrel took notice, raised an ear,
'What's so funny? I scarcely hear!'

Together they giggled, what a mess,
A duck waddled by in a bright yellow dress.
'Why tie the knot? You could just let go!'
But they winked and said, 'This is our show!'

The Magic of Connection

Two pieces of string met in the park,
Said one, 'You're bright, but I'm a bit dark.'
The other replied with a playful tease,
'Opposites attract, like ants and cheese!'

A balloon floated by, filled with delight,
'You two look tangled, but oh what a sight!'
They giggled and tangled some more in the breeze,
'Best friends forever, we're never at ease!'

Hearts in a Gentle Embrace

Two sponges met in a bubbly sea,
One said, 'Let's soak up the fun, you agree?'
They squeezed and they squished, oh what a scene,
'Together we're silly, we're soft, we're keen!'

A crab scuttled by, with a curious glance,
'You two are funny, why not do a dance?'
They wobbled and giggled, embraced in a splash,
'Here's to our friendship, it'll always last!'

Dance of Entanglement

A pair of old socks sat in a drawer,
One said, 'We're matched but I'm kind of a bore.'
The other replied, 'Let's just start a spree,
We'll twirl and we'll leap like the stars, just you see!'

Along came a shoe, with a chuckle and grin,
'You two are a riot, let the fun begin!'
They danced through the room, laughing out loud,
A sock and a shoe—who would be proud?'

Two Tracks, One Journey

Two trains on different tracks,
Chugging along, no turning back.
One's full of laughs, the other's grace,
Yet both are racing to the same place.

As they whistle loud, bump and sway,
A friendly rivalry leads the way.
Passengers giggle, popcorn in hand,
Watch the comedy unfold as they planned.

The Language of Connection

We speak in jokes, not just in lines,
A punster's dream, where laughter shines.
With silly words, we share a laugh,
Our bonds grow stronger, like a photograph.

When grumpy days come, we crack a smile,
Our friendship's a book, with each joke a mile.
Through hidden meanings and playful jest,
We learn that humor's the very best.

Threads of Affection

We weave our tales with silly yarn,
A knitted laugh can outshine a barn.
With quirky stitches and playful seams,
We create our patchwork of dreams.

Invisible strings pull us tight,
In every quirk, we find delight.
If one unravels, we'll stitch it right,
Together we shine, a comical sight.

Uniting Tides

Two waves crash in a silly spree,
Making splashes of joy, oh so carefree.
Riding high and low, what a scene,
A watery dance, like we've never seen.

Like tides that rise when laughter flows,
We surf the waves, while humor glows.
Through ebb and flow, we're forever tied,
In this playful ocean, our hearts collide.

The Color of Togetherness

When purple met the bright maroon,
They laughed and danced like it was noon.
Orange teased the shy, sweet blue,
And said, 'Let's form a funky crew!'

With stripes and dots, they played a game,
Mixing hues, without any shame.
Rainbow chuckled, what a sight,
Crafting joy from day to night.

Spirals of Affection

Around and round, the snail went slow,
Chasing the tail of a dancing crow.
'You're not as quick!' the crow did caw,
'But you're the best at making a draw!'

They twirled and spun in a spiraled chase,
Laughing together in a charming race.
When they collided, oh what a mess,
Snail wore feathers, crow wore distress!

Bound by Essence

Two little ants with grand ambitions,
Packed a picnic, ignoring conditions.
Each crumb they gathered, a morsel to share,
Creation of feasts, beyond compare.

But when the rain fell, oh what a shift,
Their lunch turned into a soggy gift.
They laughed it off, in the storm's embrace,
For adventure was worth every wet face!

Whispers of Together

The cat and dog, oh what a pair,
They schemed and plotted without a care.
'Let's catch a bird!' the dog did bark,
While the cat contemplated in the dark.

With stealthy grace, they made their move,
Only to trip, in a groovy groove.
Landing in flowers—what a surprise!
They giggled aloud, with widened eyes!

A Hearth of Unity

In a kitchen full of chaos,
The pasta's flying high,
We're stirring up a ruckus,
Like spaghetti in the sky.

The dog's wearing a chef hat,
And the cat's offering advice,
With laughter as our main dish,
We sprinkle in some spice.

Burnt toast fills the air now,
But who needs a perfect meal?
We're feasting on the giggles,
That's our secret deal.

With aprons stained and smiling,
We dance around the room,
In this lovely dish of mayhem,
Together, we'll resume.

The Essence of Togetherness

Two left feet on the dance floor,
Tripping over our own two,
But with each silly stumble,
We're finding our own groove.

With a pizza pie in hand,
And cheese stuck to our face,
We laugh at our bold moments,
In this hilarious race.

Sharing ice cream in the sun,
Melting quick, oh dear me,
But what's a little dripping,
When we're too happy to flee?

Under stars, scribbled doodles,
Our laughter fills the night,
In this goofy, crazy rhythm,
Everything feels so right.

Fabric of Forever

Stitched together with laughter,
And a few mismatched socks,
Our fabric's made of memories,
Of silly, sneaky talks.

With glue and glitter everywhere,
Crafting dreams we can wear,
We stick our hopes on paper,
While gluing down our hair.

Yet on a rainy day,
We build a fort so wide,
With snacks piled high inside,
Where our goofy spirits hide.

Every thread tells a story,
Of flaws and funny fights,
In this wild, wacky fabric,
We quilt our cozy nights.

Intertwined Journeys

On a road trip with our pals,
Maps upside down, it's true,
We missed the exit five times,
But we smiled all the way through.

Singing off-key in the car,
With snacks thrown everywhere,
We share our out-of-tune songs,
And toss our woes to air.

Getting lost in friendly banter,
Each detour makes us cheer,
Our missteps turn to laughter,
As we twirl without a fear.

At the journey's funny end,
We hold the memories dear,
In this crazy ride together,
We'll always have good cheer.

Weaving Our Echoes

In a dance of mismatched socks,
We laugh as the laundry mocks.
Twisted threads make stories bold,
In this fabric, fun to hold.

Yarn balls roll with a silly bounce,
Two left feet that fool and flounce.
Each stitch a giggle, every seam,
Together we weave our wild dream.

In the Fabric of Us

In a quilt of quirky patterns bright,
We stitch our days from morning to night.
Buttons pop, and seams may fray,
But in this chaos, we find our way.

Velcro hugs and slippery ties,
We package joy with silly cries.
Every patch tells a tale or two,
Stitched with laughter, just me and you.

Intertwined Moments

Like noodles tangled on a plate,
We intertwine and laugh at fate.
Spaghetti mishaps, a sauce parade,
In our mix, a friendship made.

Bows untie and jump around,
In this chaos, joy is found.
Our stories blend like colors bright,
In the mess, there's pure delight.

Love's Seamless Fabric

With sticky tape and glue we play,
Crafting moments, hip-hip-hooray!
Each mishap is a thread in time,
In this mess, we find our rhyme.

Sewing giggles, patching tears,
A funny dance of silly pairs.
Our fabric is a cozy blend,
Of laughter that will never end.

Unity's Embrace

In a world of mismatched socks,
We dance like quirky clocks.
Each laugh a thread, we stitch
Our lives in giggles, rich.

With every silly, wild prance,
We bring chaos to the dance.
Jellybean heartbeats race,
As we share this wobbly space.

Like spaghetti in a bowl,
We twist and stretch, we roll.
A noodle here, a twirl there,
Our friendship's quite the affair!

Together in this jest,
Life's a comedy fest.
So we paint the town bright,
With laughter holding us tight.

Interwoven Destinies

Two peas in a pod, we squish,
With every silly little wish.
Bound by giggles, high and low,
We're a circus, stealing the show.

A pancake flip, a pancake fail,
We share our stories, laugh and wail.
Twisting like a pretzel, oh so grand,
Who knew chaos was well-planned?

With our mismatched shoes, we strut,
Creating joy, no ifs or buts.
Two squirrels chasing nuts in sync,
United in our laughter's link.

So grab a fork, let's feast on fun,
Underneath the bright warm sun.
In this tapestry we weave,
We find the joy we both believe.

A Symphony of Synchronized Souls

Like a cat that always lands,
We dance with laughter in our hands.
Synchronizing every joke,
With every twist, we nearly choke.

In the kitchen, chaos reigns,
As we bounce off both our brains.
One stirs soup, the other sings,
Creating joy in silly things.

A percussion of our wacky style,
Life's a carnival, full of guile.
With harmonies of giggles sweet,
Our dorky steps can't be beat.

Let's write a song of our own tune,
Bouncing higher than the moon.
As we mash our quirky hearts,
The rhythm of laughter never departs.

Threads of Togetherness

We're like thread in a needle's eye,
Stabbing each other with every try.
But hey, it's all in fun and grace,
Stitching memories we can embrace.

Like squirrels in a nutty race,
We find the joy in every space.
So grab a cupcake, take a byte,
Our friendship is a tasty delight.

In this quilt of quirky seams,
We patch together all our dreams.
Frogs in tutus leap with glee,
Because friends make the best company.

Across the years, we spin our tale,
With every laugh, we never fail.
In this mess of life, we cheer,
For the threads that bind us near.

An Embrace of Light

In a world so bright, we do collide,
With giggles and grins, we take a ride.
We trip on hearts, like shoes untied,
Laughing together, we just can't hide.

Like fireflies dance under the moon,
We light up the night, just like a cartoon.
With silly jokes and ice cream spoons,
We navigate life, making our tunes.

Our bond's like spaghetti, twisted and fun,
One forkful, and we're never done.
With each bend and loop, we weigh a ton,
In the feast of friendship, we've already won.

Hearts Interwoven

We weave our tales like cats and yarn,
Chasing each other, we don't know harm.
With mismatched socks, our fashion's a charm,
In this clumsy dance, who knew we'd disarm?

Like peanut butter and jelly, we stick,
Navigating life, oh, what a trick!
With laughter and puns, we play our pick,
Tangled together, our hearts are thick.

In a game of charades, we're champions bold,
With gestures so wild, our secrets unfold.
You read my mind, or was that just gold?
In this crazy world, we break the mold.

The Symphony of Us

Like a duo of geese, we honk at the sun,
In this wacky rhythm, we know how to run.
With an offbeat dance, we'll never be done,
Together we laugh; oh, what a fun pun!

Our love's a concerto, quirky and bright,
With trumpets and tuba, we take flight.
In the notes of friendship, we find our light,
Singing silly songs 'til the end of night.

Like mismatched socks on laundry day,
We may be odd, but we know how to play.
In this symphony, we laugh all day,
Creating our magic in the silliest way.

Constellations of Connection

We're stars in the sky, a shimmering mess,
With cosmic giggles, we banter and jest.
Navigating orbits, we have a quest,
In this universe, we're simply blessed.

Like planets align on a Tuesday night,
We shine the brightest; it feels so right.
With each silly joke, we reach new heights,
In our galaxy, our laughter ignites.

When comets pass by, we wave hello,
In this dance of chaos, we steal the show.
From clubhouse dreams to our grand echo,
We're constellations, putting on a glow.

Infinity in Twine

In a world of knots and bows,
Two silly socks found love, who knows?
With a tangled dance of thread and lace,
They spun a yarn, a warm embrace.

A feathered hat sat on a cat,
Who twirled around with a big splat.
They giggled as they fell from grace,
A laugh together, in this wild space.

Two cups of tea, one little spout,
Shared secrets whispered, no doubt.
As the sugar stirred with joy and cheer,
It sweetened moments, bringing near.

A cupcake said, "Let's have some fun!"
While frosting danced under the sun.
With sprinkles flying, they made a mess,
In this bakery of happiness!

Joining Forces

A cookie met a glass of milk,
Together they swirled like soft silk.
Unable to stand in one place, they giggled,
As crumbs flew far, and they jiggled.

A cactus car, on the road so bright,
Wore a pair of shades, a comical sight.
With wheels that danced and squealed with glee,
They rolled along, wild and free.

A paperclip and a rubber band,
Became best pals, so in demand.
Together they held the world in check,
In an office with a quirky deck.

Balloons tied to a silly old kite,
Floated away into the night.
Their laughter echoed in the sky,
Creating joy, oh me, oh my!

Affection's Silken Path

Two spoons were nested, side by side,
In a drawer of treasures, they'd often hide.
They stirred the pot with such delight,
Creating soups that felt just right.

A silly cat chased a ball of yarn,
Fell right over with a little charm.
Purring loudly, it napped away,
In soft silks where dreams would play.

An umbrella flipped in a gusty tease,
While two rain boots danced with ease.
They leapt through puddles, big and small,
Gathering raindrops, having a ball.

A pair of mittens on a winter day,
Fought off chill in the funniest way.
Each time they slipped, they'd laugh out loud,
Bringing warmth to the snuggest crowd!

Interwoven Journeys

A pair of socks lost in the wash,
Told stories of adventures, oh so posh.
With sprinkles of dirt and a little fuzz,
Shared tales of slip-ups, just because.

A chair and a table had a chat,
About the times they'd been sat.
With crumbs of laughter and spills of tea,
They built a friendship, wild and free.

A banana peel slipped with a grin,
Led to a dance, playful spin.
As the oranges rolled, so bright and round,
They created a fruit salad profound.

A wanderer hat met a shoe's soul,
Together they aimed for a stroll.
With laughter echoing along the way,
They cherished each step, brightening the day!

Forever Knotted

In the pantry, we met,
Two socks lost in the fray.
One's striped, one's polka-dotted,
Together, they find their way.

Through laundry, they spin and dance,
A twist here, a knot there.
Who knew socks could romance?
Now they make quite the pair!

The cat, she gives a yawn,
Chasing threads in the sun.
While we watch our socks brawn,
Two peas, and so much fun.

In the drawer, they stay tight,
Comfort woven just right.
Through laughter, love does glow,
It's a match made, don't you know?

Unity's Gentle Ties

Two spoons in the drawer, you see,
One shiny, the other a bit bent.
Yet they stir up sweet memories,
Making every meal a fun event.

The forks giggle at their display,
"Come join us!" they jest with delight.
Together they brighten the day,
In this clattering kitchen of light.

Noodles twirl as if in a race,
With a wink, they share their glee.
In this chaotic, loving space,
Unity's strength is the recipe!

So toast to the mismatched crew,
In this culinary affair,
With every bite, they renew,
Their bond, they freely share!

Merging Souls

Two puzzles, lost and alone,
With pieces that just won't fit.
Yet somehow they found a home,
And now they're stuck, that's it!

The corner's a bit askew,
Edges frayed, colors collide.
But we laugh at every hue,
In our chaotic joy, we ride.

Like sandwiches made of odd stacks,
Peanut butter next to slaw.
Together we laugh and relax,
In this crazy, cosmic law.

So here's to our crooked ways,
Cherishing every bend.
With whimsy in our days,
We'll never have to pretend!

Weaving Our Story

Once a needle, sharp and spry,
Met a thread that loved to fray.
They giggled as they passed by,
And stitched life in a quirky way.

Through fabric, they slipped and slid,
A patchwork of laughter and tears.
In every quilted fabric hid,
Stories from their silly years.

Buttons popped with joy every night,
As they sewed dreams into seams.
With each tug and thrifted fight,
They knitted life with twinkling beams.

So let's embrace this odd design,
With yarn that tangles in delight.
Every loop and twist remind,
That love is silly, warm, and bright!

Threads of Shared Dreams

In the quilt of our laughter, we stitch and weave,
Life's little quirks, who'd ever believe?
With a twinkle of joy and a wink of the eye,
We share our odd tales and watch time fly.

Elastic like gum, our friendship won't snap,
With each silly jest, we both share a laugh.
Together we navigate this circus called fate,
High-fives and mishaps, oh, isn't it great?

Through tickles and tumbles, we dance on the floor,
With a twist and a turn, we keep asking for more.
In the fabric of dreams, our colors collide,
With threads made of giggles, we take it in stride.

So here's to the memories that bind us so tight,
In our witty adventures, we find pure delight.
No need for a needle, no need for a seam,
Just two friends creating a marvelous dream.

Embracing the Bond

We're like two loose screws in a wobbly chair,
One wobbles, the other's just trying to care.
In the dance of bewilderment, we spin and we sway,
Our goofball brigade laughs at life every day.

With mismatched socks and a penchant for fun,
We're the jesters of joy, always on the run.
In the folly of friendship, we've found our sweet spot,
Creating our chaos, connecting the dots.

Through the mix-ups and giggles, we share all our quirks,
Like cats in a hat, we embrace all the jerks.
A bond full of laughter, we take on the world,
Life's a wild ride, where we're joyously twirled.

So let's raise our glasses, here's to the say,
In the arms of our friendship, we'll laugh all the way.
A delightful connection, our hearts play their tune,
As we dance through this tale, under a comical moon.

Strength in Connection

We're both puzzle pieces, but missing a bit,
Fitting together, how could we not fit?
With laughter and pranks, we build our own scene,
Bringing out the sillies, our lives become keen.

Like peanut butter and jelly, we're meant to be,
In a world filled with quirks, we're the funny marquee.
Through snafus and giggles, we harness our might,
With a wink and a grin, we turn wrongs into right.

From mishaps to magic, we clear the wreckage,
In the mess of our lives, we find pure allegiance.
Together we wrestle, we tumble and roll,
Finding strength in the laughter that bonds us as whole.

So grab your popcorn, it's showtime for two,
In our circus of chaos, we'll always break through.
With a punchline and smile, we savor the ride,
In this grand little theater, we'll never divide.

Unified in Courage

In the land of the brave, we fumble and fall,
Two warriors of whimsy, we answer the call.
With a wink and a nod, we tackle the day,
Together we'll swagger, come what may.

We dress up in laughter, our capes made of cheer,
Facing life's challenges, we conquer our fear.
With fruitcake in one hand and jokes in the other,
We march on together, each sister and brother.

Through the bloopers and blunders, we rise like the sun,
In this splatter of colors, we know we're the fun.
With each twist and turn, our courage is key,
We're the knights of absurdity, wild and free.

So let's dance through the chaos, with glee in our stride,
In the carnival of life, let's take this wild ride.
With laughter our armor, we leap and we cheer,
Unified in our madness, there's nothing to fear.

The Harmony of Union

In the dance of socks on chairs,
A couple shares some goofy stares.
With laughter loud, their spirits soar,
As pizza slices hit the floor.

They argue over movie picks,
While bouncing on their favorite tricks.
A game of charades, a silly plight,
Two clowns perform in evening light.

The fridge is bare, a serious mess,
Yet smiles bloom in their shared distress.
Together they'll figure out their snacks,
In mismatched shoes and silly hats.

A journey shared, a joyful ride,
With quirks and chaos side by side.
In this wacky world where they belong,
It's laughter that carries them along.

Woven Dreams

Two pillows fight for bed space,
Each night, they join in a space race.
Mismatched sheets and laughter galore,
As they plan adventures to explore.

With socks that vanish in the wash,
They chase them down, they're in a squash.
A treasure map of items lost,
In this wild quest, it's worth the cost.

A dance-off in the kitchen space,
The spatula's their winner's grace.
With flour clouds and giggles bright,
Their kitchen battles last all night.

In cozy chaos where dreams collide,
Fun erupts, and hearts take pride.
With woven laughter, tales create,
Their silly story turns out great.

Strings of Affection

With spaghetti strings on forks they twirl,
Each bite a promise, each laugh a swirl.
They noodle dance with sauce on their chin,
Sharing culinary chaos, a tasty win!

A battle of pillows erupts at noon,
Cushions fly as they sing a tune.
Swapping jokes under sheets of blue,
With giggles flying, love feels brand new.

Doodle art on the fridge displayed,
Their silly sketches, a playful parade.
With crayons and laughter, they create their map,
In this canvas of joy, no time for a nap!

Through silly puns and playful schemes,
Life's a riot fueled by dreams.
In every chuckle, a thread is spun,
Together forever, they're having fun!

Bonds That Whisper

In quiet corners, jokes take flight,
Two pairs of sneakers, laces tight.
With whispers shared beneath the stars,
Conspiracies of chocolate bars.

They plan to prank the neighbors next,
With rubber spiders and silly texts.
Each secret laugh a silken thread,
In playful ventures, they're widely fed.

Their inside jokes a dazzling spree,
Like superheroes, wild and free.
With silly faces and goofy styles,
They light up rooms with radiant smiles.

In this circle where love's a feast,
With humor shared, they're truly released.
In every giggle, a bond that sings,
A joyful dance on love's bright wings.

Echoing Affection

In a world so vast and wide,
We giggle like a couple of kids.
Your laugh's my favorite ride,
Like two peas that sing with lids.

With every joke, a bond we weave,
Like spaghetti stuck on a wall.
Together we foolishly believe,
We can catch the moon after a fall.

Our hearts beat in a silly choir,
Dancing to a tune we made.
Like s'mores toasted by a fire,
Our sweetness never seems to fade.

So bring your quirks to my embrace,
We'll laugh until the sun sets low.
In this silly, swirling race,
We're the stars in our own show.

Hearts in Perfect Alignment

When you dance like a chicken,
And I join in with flair,
Our hearts do a spinning kitchen,
Mixing laughter in the air.

With socks that oddly never match,
We're a pair of mismatched shoes.
Love's a game that we both catch,
In ridiculousness, we choose.

From rubber chickens to silly hats,
Every moment's a sweet surprise.
With playful jabs and subtle chats,
We're two goofballs in a disguise.

In our world where oddities bloom,
You're my favorite, that's the deal.
Together we'll conquer the room,
With mirth that's wonderfully real.

The Knot of Us

We're tied with shoelaces and snacks,
Like peanut butter on jelly bread.
Our laughter fills in all the cracks,
As goofy thoughts dance in our head.

In a sea of mismatched socks,
We float like boats in the sun.
Breaking rules, like playful flocks,
Being silly is our kind of fun.

You throw me puns that make me snort,
While I trip on my own two feet.
Our love is a joyful sport,
As we compete to be the sweet.

So here's to the knots we share,
Woven in giggles without fuss.
In this dance, we make hearts rare,
Forever we are the knot of us.

Banding Together

We're like a band of silly tunes,
Harmonizing in a funny way.
Like crazy cats that dance to moons,
We find joy in every day.

With your quirks and my own flair,
We create the silliest song.
Through the ups and downs we share,
In our laughter, we belong.

So let's wear our mismatched shoes,
And prance about without a care.
In every moment, we can choose,
To be a perfect, crazy pair.

With each joke that's thrown our way,
We'll catch the fun and run away.
In this symphony of delight,
We'll band together, hearts so bright.

Bonded Threads

In a world where socks go missing,
We find our pairs in laughter's bliss,
Like mismatched shoes on a sunny day,
We dance through life, come what may.

With spaghetti noodles just like us,
Twisted and tangled without much fuss,
We share our quirks, like silly hats,
And laugh together, oh how we chat!

Like rubber bands stretched far and wide,
We snap back with a goofy pride,
In every joke, there's a strand of care,
Binding our hearts in the silly air.

So here's to bonds that are never stiff,
A life that's more like a comic riff,
With every chuckle and playful tease,
Our silly love flows like a warm breeze.

Embracing Whispers

In a world of whispers, secrets play,
We giggle quietly through the day,
With inside jokes and silly grins,
A friendship that never really thins.

We share our snacks and split our fries,
With each bite comes laughter, no goodbyes,
Like two clowns in a tiny car,
We fit together, no matter how bizarre.

Every silly dance move, every jest,
Is a sign that we are truly blessed,
With hugs that squeak and giggles that squeal,
Our bond, you see, is a giddy wheel.

So here we stand, bright spirits in tow,
With whispers of joy that steal the show,
We'll embrace the fun, come rain or shine,
In this carnival life, you're forever mine.

Knotted Souls

We're like two spoons in an oddball drawer,
Fighting for space, yet always wanting more,
With a twirl and a twist, we laugh and cry,
Our knots of mishaps never run dry.

In the great circus of life's wild ride,
We juggle dreams with a humorous pride,
With pies in the face and pranks galore,
Our friendship's a riot, who could ask for more?

Like gum on a shoe, we stick together,
Through storms and sunshine, no matter the weather,
With each silly pun that makes us grin,
These knotted souls are bound to win.

So let's embrace every tangled part,
With a laugh, we bare our foolish heart,
In this wacky journey, let's never fret,
For our knotted souls are the best duet!

Unity of Stars

In this galaxy of quirky sights,
We shine like stars on the longest nights,
With giggles that echo through the cosmic dance,
Every awkward moment gives us a chance.

Like constellations drawing silly maps,
We navigate life with belly laughs,
With every wish on a shooting star,
Our union sparkles, no matter how far.

With moonlit shadows and bright sun rays,
We paint the dark in the funnest ways,
Together we roast marshmallows absurdly,
As we float on dreams, ever so curdly.

So here's to the laughter, the twinkling fun,
Our unity shines, oh what a run!
Through comets and laughter, we'll always stay,
In the universe's embrace, come what may.

Pledges in Thread

We promised with shoelaces, tied in a knot,
Eloped in a thimble, forgot what we bought.
A yarn ball of secrets, we spun with glee,
Two goofs wrapped in fabric, how silly we be!

With buttons for eyes, we giggled and cheered,
Socks mismatched but warm, no worries or fears.
Knitting our dreams with a clumsy old purl,
While crafting our quirks, we'd give it a whirl.

A patch on our pants, a spot on the floor,
We laugh like the loons, oh what could be more?
In stitches together, like puppets on strings,
Oh, the joy that this haphazard sewing can bring!

So grab your needle, let's start this grand dance,
With threads of absurdity, give love a chance.
Together we'll tumble, like yarn in a spin,
With fabric and folly, let the fun begin!

Love's Unbreakable Chains

Locked in a closet, we giggled and played,
With silly old handcuffs that never obeyed.
Chained by our laughter, we craved for some cheese,
Woven together by foolish degrees!

Oh, love is a tether, not meant to confine,
Like cats in a basket, all tangled in twine.
Frying our friendship like eggs on the side,
With beats that we dance to, our hearts open wide.

We huddle like kittens, all stuck in a jam,
Made goofy connections, oh my, what a slam!
With each funny moment, we grow a bit stronger,
Like chains made of giggles, they surely last longer.

Mismatched and messy, it's what we adore,
With chains made of laughter, who could ask for more?
Though tangled and twisted, we gladly abide,
In bonds that are silly, side by side we reside!

Cherished Entwinements

Two spoons in a drawer, forever are wed,
Baking our memories, frosting some bread.
Twisted like pretzels, our paths intertwined,
A dance that is goofy, in rhythms unrefined.

With candy-coated dreams, we scissors and tape,
Gluing our giggles, like glue we escape.
Our hearts like balloons, they float and they sway,
In chaos and laughter, we find our own way.

Wrapped up like mummies, no way to get free,
Giggles erupting, just you wait and see!
Entwined in this dance, we're flickering bright,
Two flames in the darkness, we light up the night.

Through spaghetti and meatballs, we muddle and mix,
With absurd little jokes, we flourish and fix.
Here's to our journey, so wobbly and fun,
With cherished entwinements, we shine like the sun!

The Spiral of Affection

Like pasta in water, we swirl and we spin,
In circles of laughter, where do we begin?
From fettuccine dreams to cavatappi plans,
Our hearts like a whirlpool, we dance in a trance.

We noodle and giggle, we frolic and twirl,
Through the sauce of our hopes, our imaginations swirl.
In the pot of affection, we're simmering slow,
With a dash of nonsense and a sprinkle of glow.

Tickling moments like fettuccine strands,
Whipping up joy with our quirky hands.
In the kitchen of chaos, we feast when we play,
With a spiral of magic that brightens our day.

So let's make a feast with this love that we share,
Stirring up laughter, with the utmost care.
In this spiral of friendship, we'll twirl around tight,
Creating a banquet of pure delight!

Shadows of Together

In a world of mismatched shoes,
We trip and fall with silly views.
Dancing awkward, left and right,
Our giggles echo through the night.

Two spoons in a single bowl,
Chasing cereal is the goal.
The milk splashes, we burst out loud,
In our chaos, we're so proud.

With tangled hair and morning sighs,
We bake together, what a surprise!
Flour flies, with laughter each scoop,
Our kitchen's now a baking troop.

A selfie fail, we strike a pose,
With silly faces, that's how it goes!
Together we shine, a comic delight,
In this goofy world, we're alright.

Links of Love

In a game of twisted charades,
You mimic me, and I'm amazed!
Your antics crack me up all night,
As we dance like we're taking flight.

Two peas in a pod, that's what they say,
But we're more like a comedy play.
With puns and jokes, we laugh and grin,
In this silly loop, let the fun begin!

Choosing snacks, the greatest feat,
Who ate my chips? This isn't neat!
A pillow fight, we both take aim,
Feathers fly; oh, what a game!

Through ups and downs, we share the jest,
Side by side, it's simply the best.
With silly faces, we take the stage,
In our funny tale, we'll never age.

Heartstrings in Harmony

You sing off-key, yet I join in,
Our rhythm might as well just spin.
With hiccups, giggles, and misplaced beats,
We create sunshine on stormy streets.

Strumming guitars made of paper clips,
We're rock stars with our funny quips.
The cat joins in, a howling friend,
Together, our silliness won't end.

Chasing rainbows with ketchup on fries,
In our world, no room for goodbyes.
Throwing confetti on spaghetti nights,
Life's better with these silly sights.

With each adventure, the laughter swells,
Creating stories that no one sells.
In harmony, we spin and swirl,
Just two goofs, giving life a twirl.

Echoes of the Joined

In a room full of mismatched socks,
We're searching high and low, what a shock!
You wear my favorite, I wear yours,
Life's so funny, it simply soars.

With whipped cream fights and pie in the face,
Who knew love could be such a race?
Giggles burst from every corner,
As we become our own sweet mourner.

Tickling tales in a bedtime chat,
I told the cat, you told the brat.
With each whisper, the chuckles grow,
In our funny world, we steal the show.

Two hearts in sync, sharing our glee,
Wrapped in laughter, wild and free.
Together forever in a joyful spree,
With echoes of fun, just you and me.

Echoes of Entwined Dreams

In a world of mismatched socks,
We giggle over tangled clocks.
You steal my fries, I take your drink,
Our laughter's louder than we think.

Pet gerbils race in backward sprints,
We place our bets on silly hints.
From wobbly chairs, we spill our tea,
A circus show for you and me.

Dancing shadows, silly hats,
Waltzing clumsily with the cats.
With every trip, a joyful scream,
Together we're a funny dream.

So let the world spin where it may,
In our own whirl, we wrestle play.
Through thick and thin, with joyful cheer,
We'll dance our way to every year.

Bonds that Dance

In mismatched shoes, our feet collide,
A two-step tango, joy can't hide.
We trip and fall, yet hear no sound,
In laughter's grip, our hearts are found.

On roller skates, we swerve and bump,
Your ice cream drips, then makes a plump.
With every silly, sticky mess,
Our goofy ways, we both confess.

Umbrella fights on rainy days,
Soaked to the skin, in funny ways.
We'll splash through puddles, full of glee,
And dance like fools, just you and me.

So let's crazy-dance in perfect sync,
With joyful chaos, hearts won't shrink.
Life is a party, come join the chance,
In every moment, our bonds will dance.

A Tapestry of Us

In a patchwork quilt of silly threads,
We stitch our laughs, ignore the dreads.
With glue all over, we craft our days,
Creating chaos in fun-filled ways.

A fruit fight here, a pie-face there,
Your sneaky grins, I can't despair.
With flickering candles, we share a cake,
Each bite a giggle, no chance to break.

Clumsy hands throw confetti bright,
While our dance moves capture the sight.
Paint splatters tell our crazy tale,
Together we laugh, we never fail.

A jigsaw fit, with edges frayed,
In every goof-up, love is displayed.
So here we weave, both strong and free,
A tapestry stitched with jubilee.

Chords of Affection

With ukuleles and banjo strings,
Our playlist's filled with silly things.
A twist of fate, a wobbly beat,
Makes every note a joyful feat.

Sing off-key, who cares for sound?
Our melodies are joy unbound.
In silly duets, we voice our dreams,
Like cats that croon in moonlit beams.

A symphony made of hearts so light,
We giggle and dance till the sun's bright.
With every strum, we break the norm,
Our hearts a chorus, forever warm.

So here's to love, with laughter's grace,
In goofy rhythms, we find our place.
Together we'll play until the end,
In every chord, you are my friend.

Unity in Every Stitch

In a quilt of friends, we sew with glee,
Each patch a tale, as wild as can be.
With threads of laughter, bright colors we pick,
Stitching our quirks, it's a hilarious trick!

A button here, a zipper there,
Sewing up joy, without a care.
We've needle fights and yarn wars too,
A fabric of fun, that's our crew!

When life unravels, we gather near,
Patching up woes with a dose of cheer.
Our seams may fray, but oh what a sight,
In this crazy quilt, everything feels right!

So raise your scissors, and let's toast,
To the stitches that bind us, we love the most.
No fabric softener can wash away,
The joy we weave in our wacky display!

Love's Intricate Weave

With magic fingers, we twist the thread,
Making mischief instead of dread.
We weave our dreams where nonsense collides,
Tangled in giggles, our joy never hides!

In the loom of life, we dance a jig,
Crafting our tales, both bold and big.
Using sticky tape and a little glue,
We fix our hiccups, me and you!

Watch out for yarn balls rolling around,
Tripping up laughter, oh what a sound!
Our patterns are wacky, like socks gone rogue,
In this fabric fiesta, we're in full vogue!

Together we craft, with chaos and care,
Creating our story, a tapestry rare.
Every loop and twirl, tells a tale so bright,
We're the weavers of joy, shining in the light!

Bonds Beyond Measure

With rubber bands and a dash of flair,
We clasp our bonds, floating in the air.
Like spaghetti tangled on a dinner plate,
Our friendship's a dance, never second-rate!

We measure our laughs with rulers and glee,
Counting all moments, one, two, and three.
Each giggle a stretch, each smile a loop,
We're an odd bunch, our own merry troop!

From paper clips to silly string,
Our creations make the heart take wing.
In this wild game of connect the dots,
We find joy in the chaos, not in the knots!

So here's to the bonds, both silly and true,
That pull us together, like glue on a shoe.
Our friendship's a measure of goofiness grand,
With laughter and love, always hand in hand!

Hearts Interlaced in Harmony

In a circus of joy, we juggle and sing,
Interlacing laughter, what fun we bring!
With each little giggle, a ring we create,
A tangled duet that just can't wait!

We're cartwheeling through days, what a sight to see,
With hearts like confetti, wild and free.
Each moment a spark, like fireworks above,
We're an oddball orchestra, playing for love!

Our rhythm's a dance of tangled delight,
Wrapping around each other so tight.
Playing hopscotch on dreams so wide,
In this wacky opera, we take pride!

So let's twirl together, a kaleidoscope spree,
With mismatched socks, you and me.
In this symphony of goofy and grand,
Harmony reigns when we hold hands!

Strings of Connection

In a world of tangled threads,
Laughter weaves through every dread.
We trip and fall, then stand up tall,
Our silly dance, a joyful call.

With rubber bands and paper clips,
We sail on ships of friendship trips.
A group of clowns in silly hats,
Creating chaos, what's wrong with that?

Through jumbled yarn and mismatched socks,
Together we compose, tick-tock.
A symphony of laughs we hum,
Our ties are strong, let joy become.

A Quilt of Memories

Stitched with giggles and warm delight,
Every patch tells tales at night.
An old sock here, a button there,
Quirky patterns, a funny wear.

With every fold, a story's spun,
Of clumsy falls and silly fun.
We quilt our lives through every seam,
In the fabric of laughter, we gleam.

The pets have joined, they're part of this,
With fur and fluff, nothing is amiss.
Catch a loose thread, give it a tug,
And watch all our memories snug as a bug.

Fusion of Souls

Like mashed potatoes and sweet gravy,
We blend together, feeling wavy.
A sprinkle of joy, a dash of cheer,
In this wild mix, we hold what's dear.

With giant spoons and silly hats,
We're crafting dreams like clever brats.
A fusion dance, a joyful flair,
With laughter floating through the air.

We're spice and sugar, salt and lime,
In whimsical ways, we share our time.
A recipe for joy, we mull,
In this big pot, our hearts are full.

The Embrace of Together

Like a warm hug from a big teddy bear,
We squeeze each other, show we care.
A tickle here, a pinch right there,
In a giggling storm, we freely share.

With open arms and silly grins,
We dance like fools and spin like winds.
In our silly embrace, time stands still,
The joy we find is quite the thrill.

So wrap me up in your laughter bright,
Together we'll face the dark of night.
For in this hug, we find the key,
A bond unbroken, you and me.

Woven Wishes

In a fabric store, we met one day,
Threading our dreams in a silly way.
Laughed at the patterns, colors galore,
Stitching up laughter, we couldn't ignore.

Then tangled our yarns, oh what a mess!
A scarf of giggles we tried to dress.
With every loop, we could hardly breathe,
Creating a quilt where joy wouldn't leave.

Dancing with needles, we made quite a scene,
Knit one, purl two, what does it mean?
But every mishap just made us cheer,
Our woven wishes drew us near.

So here's to the threads that pull us tight,
In stitches and snickers, everything's right.
A tapestry of fun that we both can wear,
Forever entwined, a whimsical pair.

The Connection Within

Two socks in a dryer, a spin and a whirl,
One from the left and one from the girl.
Tangled together, they giggle and sway,
A perfect duo, in their own funny way.

Bouncing in laughter, they tumble about,
Who knew that pairing could lead to a shout!
In mismatched patterns, they flaunt their fun,
A sock unity, they've already won!

They scheme and they dream of adventures bright,
To dance all night without any fright.
In sudsy waters, their bond grew thick,
Just two little fellows, a real magic trick!

So let's raise a toast to pals of the spin,
In the wild world of socks, they both fit in.
For it's not just the pairs that make us grin,
It's the connections we find, deep within!

Emblem of Togetherness

In a park where the squirrels frolic and play,
Two birds met one sunny, bright day.
One said 'Tweet' while the other said 'Cheep',
Together they chirped, a chorus so sweet.

They spun 'round a branch like a carnival ride,
A swirl of feathers, oh what a sight!
Their laughter echoed through chirps and through calls,
An emblem of togetherness that joyfully sprawls.

Every silly wiggle and flip in the air,
Brought giggles from passers, a wonderful flare.
They snickered at owls who chewed on their lunch,
In their feathery dance, they packed quite a punch!

So here's to the twosome, a comedic pair,
Creating a ruckus without any care.
In a world of wonders, they stole the show,
Squeaking delight in the sun's warm glow!

Harmony in Every Loop

In a circus tent, a clown and a bear,
Made a grand duet, quite a peculiar pair.
Juggling with pies, not a care in the world,
With giggles and gaffes, their antics unfurled.

The clown threw a pie, the bear wore a grin,
With whipped cream and laughter, they both jumped in.
Tumbling together, they'd dance and they'd bop,
With a twirl and a spin, they just couldn't stop.

Together they balanced on one tiny ball,
With wiggles and shakes, they delighted us all.
Oh, the harmony found in twists and in loops,
Brought happiness bursting in giggling groups!

So let's cheer for the bond, laughter's sweet call,
In the circus of life, their love conquers all.
For the moments we share, hilarious and bright,
Are the loops that connect us, a shared delight!

An Alliance of Spirits

In a world of quirky dreams,
Where laughter flows like streams,
We juggled thoughts with a grin,
And began our playful spin.

With rubber bands and silly glue,
We crafted bonds that grew and grew,
Like a game of hopscotch on a hill,
Our friendship blooms, it gives a thrill.

We share our snacks and silly jokes,
Amidst the chaos, there's no hoax,
With every quirk and little quip,
We sail through life on a friendship ship.

So raise your glass, let laughter soar,
In this alliance, who could ask for more?
With every giggle and silly cheer,
We've stitched our hearts, let's grab a beer!

Entanglement of Paths

Two clumsy souls on a winding road,
With mismatched shoes and a heavy load,
We tripped on fate and laughed so loud,
In this chaos, we feel so proud.

A mismatched puzzle, we fit just right,
Sharing ice cream on a pink-swirled night,
Our jokes are like ties with a bow,
In each stumble, our laughter will grow.

We danced with umbrellas in summer rain,
Sang silly songs on the back of a train,
With every twist and a turn to explore,
We tangled paths, wanting more.

So let's forge ahead with grins so wide,
In this amusing roller coaster ride,
With every step, we'll be side by side,
Our connection, where joy and fun abide!

Fables of Unity

Once upon a time, in a land of cheer,
Where giggles ruled, and there's nothing to fear,
We spun tales of friendship, oh so grand,
With every word, we held a hand.

A cat that danced with a goofy hat,
And a dog who dreamed of being a brat,
In silly fables, our spirits would rise,
Crafting connections in laughs and sighs.

With oops and whews, we'd stumble through,
Finding joy in the little things we do,
In this funny tapestry we weave,
There's magic in every laugh we believe.

So gather 'round, let the stories unfold,
With every chuckle, we break the mold,
In these fables of unity, we find our place,
A tapestry woven, full of grace!

Dances of Connection

In the rhythm of laughter, we sway and spin,
With two left feet, yet we always win,
We whirl through life in clumsy delight,
Creating memories that shine so bright.

The floor is our canvas, our shuffles the paint,
Each silly dance move without a restraint,
In this waltz of friendship, we take the lead,
Our bond's like a song, it plants a seed.

With twirls and giggles, we jump and hop,
From laughter's cradle, we never stop,
In every misstep, we find our groove,
In this dance, our spirits move.

So let the music play, let's laugh and frolic,
In perfect connection, so bright and iconic,
With every pirouette, we lift each other high,
In this humorous dance, watch our spirits fly!

A Dance of Souls

In a ballroom of giggles, we sway,
With two left feet, we dance, hooray!
You step on my toes, I don't mind,
This goofy rhythm, so well defined.

A spin and a twirl, we laugh so loud,
Our shadows mingle, like a happy crowd.
You flip and I flop, and... oh, what a sight!
Two stars colliding in the silly night.

In a whirl of confetti and dreams,
We tangle our laughter, bursting at seams.
With every step, we're a joyful mess,
After all, it's the fun that we bless.

So let's clap our hands and stomp our feet,
In this frolicsome dance, oh what a treat!
As we slip and we slide, let's create a show,
In this quirky ballet, the best place to go!

Entangled Destinies

In a web of mishaps, we intertwine,
Like spaghetti noodles, in pasta divine.
You drop your ice cream, I spill my drink,
Together we giggle, what do you think?

We chase after pigeons, they take to the sky,
We run in circles, oh me, oh my!
Your hat flies away, my shoe's untied,
In this circus of chaos, let's take it in stride.

Like two comets zipping in space,
We wobble and fumble, quicken the pace.
With every misstep, we find our groove,
In this dance of blunders, we must approve.

So join hands, dear friend, don't look so glum,
Our lives are a carnival, a whacky drum!
We're tangled together in giggles and cheer,
Let's embrace our oddity, year after year!

Kinship of Spirits

In a land of odd socks and mismatched shoes,
We march to the rhythm of silly blues.
With wobbly waves and a feathery cheer,
Our spirits connect, loud and clear.

We build castles from pillows, oh what a sight,
Defending our fort from a phantom knight.
You throw a marshmallow, I duck just in time,
In our kingdom of nonsense, we reign in our prime.

Like two peas in a pod, we're quirks at their best,
In every adventure, we put laughter to test.
With each silly joke and each playful tease,
We dance through the chaos, aiming to please.

So let's share our secrets, our giggles, our dreams,
In this whirlwind of life, we make silly schemes.
Together we wander, hand in hand through the fun,
In our kinship of spirits, we're never outdone!

Hand in Hand Across Time

With time on our side and snacks by the bay,
We embark on adventures, come what may.
From wiggle to waddle, we leap and we bound,
In our silly journey, joy knows no ground.

Like dinosaurs dancing in mismatched clothes,
We frolic through ages, everyone knows.
With laughter as fuel and friendship as glue,
We mesh through the moments, just me and you.

In a time machine made of candy and fright,
We zoom through the ages, what a delight!
With giggles and hiccups, we chase the sun,
In this merry chase, we're always outrun.

So hand in hand, let's sprint into week,
Through corridors of fun, there's no need to sneak.
Our timeline is wobbly, with joy and delight,
Forever together, we'll dance through the night!

The Weft of Togetherness

In a world of tangled yarn,
We knit our jokes with glee.
Stitching laughter into fabric,
Who knew love was so tacky?

Knots that squirm and twist about,
Like cats on a sunny day.
We patch the holes with giggles,
And chase the blues away.

With popcorn strings and silly strings,
We dance through life's buffet.
Each mashup of our whimsies,
Turns drab into cabaret.

From mismatched socks to silly hats,
Our threads will never fray.
In this patchwork quilt we bond,
Awkward beats lead the ballet.

Embracing the Ties

We embrace with goofy grins,
Like two koalas in a tree.
Our hugs are wrapped in laughter,
A quirky jubilee.

With every bobble, every laugh,
We waltz a clumsy jig.
The more we trip and tumble,
The bigger grows our gig.

Each pun's a playful nudge,
That keeps us side by side.
With each knocked-over coffee cup,
We share the drips of pride.

In this game of catch and tickle,
We find our rhythm sweet.
Our hearts may dance a polka,
But our love's a funky beat.

Merging Paths

Two paths crossed in clumsy style,
Like big feet on small toes.
We navigate this crazy life,
With slips and snorts and woes.

Our journeys twist and turn around,
Like spaghetti on a plate.
Each fork may lead to mayhem,
But oh, it's worth the wait!

With every goofy pun we share,
We merge in laughter bright.
Together we're an oddball team,
In this wacky, wild flight.

Side by side in this big mess,
We spark the joy we need.
Whether on a pogo stick,
Or chasing down a seed.

Cherished Bonds

There's a glue made out of smiles,
And some sprinkles of delight.
We stick together effortlessly,
Even when we want to fight.

In our world of silly faces,
Every snort's a shared embrace.
A dance-off in the kitchen,
Keeps us in the happy race.

We're like cookies with odd flavors,
A mix of sweet and spice.
Our bond, a generous recipe,
Nothing's ever too precise.

So here's to all our silly times,
With love and laughs galore.
Together in our joyful mess,
Forever we'll explore.

www.ingramcontent.com/pod-product-compliance
Lightning Source LLC
Chambersburg PA
CBHW070004300426
43661CB00141B/207